The Gift of His Embrace

By Judy Carson

Judy Carson

The Gift of His Embrace
By Judy Carson

To Barbara
Your support, understanding and belief in me made it possible for me to find my "voice" and gave me the courage I needed to complete this book. Thank you so much for being my number one cheerleader and always encouraging me to be more than I think I can be.

1

They came in all sizes, all shapes, all colors, and even all ages. Lines and lines of people all patiently waiting their turn. No one is pushing and shoving trying to get a better spot or a better view. No one is trying to cut in line. There is no sheer chaos like when the doors at the mall open on the first "official" Christmas shopping day. There is no fear of running out of the latest Tommy Hilfiger jeans or not getting the last Cabbage Patch doll. No one is arguing or fighting, making rude comments, spreading gossip or rumors; no derogatory comments being said just loud enough to "accidentally" be overheard by their target.

No matter how far back in line you are, you have a perfect view of the front of the line. It's as clear as if you were the next person. It is a better view than even the best jumbo-tran screen at any stadium or concert.

You don't care how long the line is, you are content to wait. It will be worth the wait no matter how long that may be. In fact, with thousands and thousands of people gathered, it actually is peaceful, calm, quiet and serene. What could draw such a crowd, you ask. The answer is simple — He can.

There is no obnoxious "elevator music" ringing out through loud speakers. In fact, there are no speakers or sound systems whatsoever. What? No speakers? No sound system? How is that possible? You can hear Him speak as clearly as if you were face-to-face. He doesn't shout or raise His voice, but as each person goes to leave, you hear Him say, "I love you so much. Come back soon," and you can tell by the look in His eyes that He means it. Odd, how that is the only part of the conversations you can hear.

As I stand in line, my mind begins to wander and takes me back to a time long since forgotten; a time when the holidays were filled with excitement and wonder; a time when most parents looked forward to taking their children to see Santa Claus. Why did they look forward to it? Because they knew that once their children had the chance to sit on Santa's lap, life would be much less stressful for the next four weeks. Everyone knows that Santa keeps a list of all the boys and girls and he knows if they have been bad or good. Once children sit on Santa's lap and are reminded that he will be watching and that he knows if they are being good, they are going to be on their best behavior. If they should forget and begin to cause problems or act up, you can bet their mom or dad will be quick to refresh their memory.

As I begin thinking about that time in my life, I find myself feeling rather melancholy. I was always a pretty good kid. I didn't need Santa coming to town for me to behave properly. I was always going out of my way to please, to help, and to make my mom happy. I was a good little girl, but never good enough. It didn't matter how good my grades were, it was always the lowest grade that was noticed. If I were to try and surprise Mom and do the dusting, she always noticed the spot I missed or the table I forgot to do. The fact that the rest of the furniture looked great went unnoticed.

I remember a couple years of being thrilled to go see Santa. I would count the days until he was coming to town. Our small town didn't have a mall, so Santa would usually come to our fire station. He would ride into town on a big, red fire truck. I would lie in bed at night and think of what to put on my list. I would write and rewrite it in my head over and over again. What should I tell him? What did I really want more than anything? What was it ok to ask for? As I would think about that last question, my list would become shorter and shorter. After several years of being afraid to ask for much of anything, and then not getting it anyway, the idea of going to see Santa Claus lost most of its excitement.

I learned quickly that it wasn't ok to want things. Asking for anything was frowned upon.

"Manners" not only included "please" and "thank you" but politely refusing things offered to me as well. If I was at someone's house and they offered me a piece of candy then I should say "no, thank you." If I was told I could have a piece, then I was definitely only to take one piece and be sure to say thank you. This didn't just apply to sweets or treats but to other situations as well. If a friend were to offer me one of her toys because she wanted me to have it, I was to politely refuse. Sometimes telling a friend I liked their bike or their sled would be enough to cause problems at home. Such a simple statement would be interpreted as me implying I wanted it, and like I said, it wasn't ok to want things. If there was something you really wanted, you definitely weren't supposed to tell anybody what it was. That would be totally selfish! A good girl would be perfectly happy with whatever she got! After all, money didn't grow on trees and Santa had a lot of people to get things for. I should be happy that he would take the time to stop and give me anything at all. To want or to think I deserved more than what I got was to be greedy. And greed was NOT a good thing! Greed was bad and people who were greedy were bad people.

One Christmas, however, I did get Rock-'em-Sock- 'em Robots! That was one of my best Christmases ever! I must have been particularly good that year to deserve something like that! As I thought about these things, I was caught off-guard by a tear trickling down my cheek. Wow! Where did that come from? I hadn't been aware of having any feelings regarding my childhood years in such a long time. So long in fact, it felt like a lifetime ago!

Of course, in some ways it was a lifetime ago. I can't remember the last time I experienced any emotional reaction to things from my past. Things were different then; I was different. To say that I was a person who wasn't in-touch with her feelings would be an understatement. I had spent years trying to avoid or forget the past. I would view my childhood through rose-colored glasses to see it in a brighter light. This was easy to do since I also had very few memories of that time in my life. Memories and feelings were locked up together in a secret hiding place and I had thrown that key away. Some things were better left unknown, and who needed feelings anyways?

2

Just then I am bumped from behind and hear a commotion. A young woman and her two children are behind me. The children are getting restless. I can tell the woman is feeling overwhelmed and is not sure how to handle her children's restlessness. They aren't being bad; they are just tired, and I can tell that they have about reached their limit of just standing in line. They are ready to run and play. The little boy, who appears to be the oldest, seems to think that teasing his sister and running around her is a good use of his time. Obviously, his sister and mother don't agree with this. The mother raises her voice to try to rein in her son and suddenly remembers where she is. She instantly lowers her voice and begins to cry.

My heart goes out to the woman. I have no idea what I would do if I were in a similar situation. I offer her a kleenex, and as I hand it to her, I also offer her my place in line. She looks at me in disbelief. It is only one spot, but the look on her face would make you think that one spot made miles of difference. She tries to graciously decline, but as she does I just casually sidestep around her and get back in line behind her. She thanks me as she continues to wipe her eyes. I chat with her son about sports and athletes that he likes, (hoping I can at least provide a distraction and give his mom a few more minutes to settle down). The line continues to move and as it does the woman picks up her little girl and hugs her.

"I love you so much. Come back soon," I hear the Man say again. As I look up, the line inches forward as another person walks away, her face all aglow. Soon, she disappears in the crowd. I watch as the Man aids the next person, an elderly gentleman, up the steps. He is patient and pleasant. The elderly man looks a bit skeptical and hesitant. He stands there, looking at the ground. As I watch, I see the Man gently lift the old man's chin to look him in the eyes. I am still too far away to hear what is being said, but as I watch the expression on the Man's face it is obvious He is concerned for the elderly man and is moved with compassion. The elderly man begins to cry as they talk. He seems so sad and broken. The Man gently wipes the other man's tears, draws him to Himself and holds him. When they are through, they both bow their heads in prayer. With one more hug, again I hear Him say, "I love you so much. Come back soon." As the elderly man leaves, he smiles as he wipes away the last of his tears.

The line keeps moving. Some people seem to only be up there for a minute or two. Other people are there a lot longer. It doesn't appear to make any difference to the Man. He treats each person compassionately regardless of how much time each takes. It isn't as if He rushes some through but lingers with others. You can tell that the people in line and what brought them here determines the amount of time He gives to each person. Even though many walk away in tears, no one seems to be upset or disappointed as they leave. All of them have the same glow on their faces.

Suddenly, trouble starts in the line. People are pushing and someone is yelling. Hearing the noise, the Man stands. "Children," He says, "Please, everyone will have a chance to speak with Me. I have no intention of sending anyone away without spending time with you. You all are very important to Me, and it disturbs Me to see you treating each other rudely. I know you have been here a long time. If you are tired of waiting you can leave, but I really hope you decide to be patient and wait." The people in line calm down. I don't know if it is what He said, the gentleness in His voice, or the look in His eyes. It is a mixture of compassion, righteousness and authority, but yet not offensive. In fact, it is inviting.

As things calm down, once again I find myself thinking about my childhood. I don't remember much about that time in my life, only bits and pieces here and there. I have no memories of sitting around the dinner table sharing about our day. No memories of rushing home from school to find Mom waiting for us with a plate of brownies fresh out of the oven, eager to hear how school was. No memories of joyous holidays or birthdays. In fact, I don't have any birthday memories at all. The one thing I remember is that on our birthday we got to choose where we wanted to have our birthday dinner. I would generally choose a Chinese restaurant, not only because I liked Chinese food but because I also knew it was my mom's favorite.

I find myself wondering why I didn't have any memories about those times. Should I add that to my wish list? I wonder. Not what you would call a "typical" wish. But then this list of wants is definitely a different sort of list. This line isn't about the newest toys or latest hi-tech gadgets. It has nothing to do with the wildest fashions, flat screen televisions or smart phones. So what is it all these people would stand in line for? It isn't to try out for a reality show or to be a contestant on a game show. No! These people are here for something much different. They are here in response to a “universal” question: “what do you want?”

It’s astounding how difficult that question is for me. It seems like a rather simple, straight-forward question; what do you want? What do I want? Do I know? Have I ever known? Oh sure, there have been times when I knew what I wanted. For instance, when I was eight or nine years old, I wanted a German Shepherd puppy. We got a Doberman. Or when I wanted us to stay in Spencerville but instead we moved to Alverado so my sister could have a horse. So there have been times I’ve thought about it, but it just never seemed to matter what I wanted. Evidently, not only was it wrong to want something, but wanting something seemed to me to be a good way to guarantee I wouldn’t get it. This led to a very bleak outlook on life, plus left me feeling unimportant. After awhile, I just stopped wanting or wishing for much of anything. Jimminy

Cricket had it all wrong; it really does make a difference who you are when wishing upon a star for those dreams to come true. So what do I want? I find myself asking myself that question a lot lately, especially since getting the invitation to come here today. I considered declining the invitation, but there was no contact information and no R.S.V.P. The invitation was rather simple. It gave a place, a day and a time. It's what it said on the front that intrigued me, however.

> Ever feel like you were worthless? Invisible? Unheard? Unseen? Not needed? Unimportant? Any or all of the above? If you could have anything in the world that you desired, what would it be?
>
> Please accept this open invitation to come and meet with Me and learn your true value. Don't believe the lies! None of the above is true! Come to Me. I long for you. Talk to Me.

I truly want to hear what you have to say.
Don't be afraid! It's time you were heard!
Allow Me to fulfill your greatest desire, grant your wildest dream and meet your most desperate need.
I want to do this for you. But it's up to you.
All you have to do is come to the designated place on the given date. I will do the rest

Too good to be true? Try Me! What do you want? Just come and let Me know. I long to give it to you. You won't be disappointed.
I look forward to seeing you soon."

Actually, I threw the invitation away. It sounded too much like a set-up to me. "Too good to be true" didn't even come close to describing how impossible and impractical it sounded. Nobody could offer such a thing! There was no way this was legitimate! It had to be a hoax, but who would do that to me? The fear of it being true overwhelmed me. It was just too much to hope for. I couldn't risk it! It would be better to just ignore the invitation and never know if it was true. As the days went by, I began to ask myself, "What if it's true? What if this isn't some cruel hoax? What do you have to lose?" Actually, I believed I could lose a great deal. To allow myself to hope was to risk losing everything. Hope didn't come easy to me. I had no idea who sent the invitation. How could I trust this to be real when there was no name on it? I struggled daily with trusting the people I knew. The risk and the fear paralyzed me, but I couldn't get away from the thought of "what if?" I decided that I would come, but not expecting much. More like an observer. I never imagined there would be this many people. No one could have sent out this many invitations! So where did all these people come from?

3

Suddenly, a tap on my shoulder startles me. "Excuse me, but the line is moving," the man behind me says. I notice there is a gap between the woman with her two children who are in front of me and myself. The children are quiet now, each holding on to their mother's shirttail. Evidently the line has moved up while I was lost in my thoughts and I have fallen a bit behind. I quickly make up the ground and am back in place. I begin overhearing pieces of conversations of people around me. Everyone seems to still be trying to figure out what he or she will ask for or what it is they really need to be able to say to someone. Many seem to be skeptical and hesitant to want to wish too big for fear of not getting it and being let down. Most people seem to be considering asking for things like improved health issues for themselves or a loved one; healings; restored relationships; improved communication skills; a college degree;

a better education; a good job; a loving family; and some just want to be wanted. Others have grandiose ideas of money, possessions and property that they will ask for. They believe in asking and asking big. That concept just seems so wrong to me! How can anyone be so selfish and greedy? Fortunately, the people thinking about wealth and possessions seem to be the minority. I have to wonder, is it truly wrong to want such things? I begin to realize that the reason I believe it is wrong is because I was raised to believe that. But what if it really is all right to want to be rich?

My family wasn't poor but we were far from wealthy. I can't remember a time when we had to go without food or school clothes or a house to live in. The basic essential needs were always met. I had always believed that was enough, which was all anyone truly needed. If that was true, why did it seem so much of what I desperately needed as I was growing up was missing? Could I have been wrong about this all these years? If so, what would that mean? What is it I truly want? What is it that I needed as a child that I didn't get? Why is it that there seems to be so much that I missed out on in childhood? Why don't I remember? Most of these questions are new to me. Never have I questioned my upbringing. I am an intelligent, polite, well-mannered woman and had always been a rather well-behaved little girl. I turned out fairly well. Or did I? If that were true, then why is it I have spent most of my life wishing I were dead? That doesn't sound like the wish of someone whose "basic essential needs" were met.

I ponder these questions as the line continues to move. It has been a long day. As I wonder how long I have been here it occurs to me that it is still daylight. How can that be? I have been in line for what seems like an entire day, yet the sun is still out. It is a beautiful day! Not too hot or cold. There is a gentle breeze blowing. You couldn't have asked for a nicer day for this sort of thing. Time seems to be standing still for this event.

I look around me and it seems as if people are still coming. The lines look just as long now as when I arrived hours earlier, but I can tell that I am getting much closer to the front of the line. The closer I get, the more my tension and the excitement rise. It is mixed with much apprehension on my part. Even though nobody seems to leave disappointed, I still have to wonder if this is for real. Can this man fulfill my greatest desire? Can He grant my wildest dream? Whereas earlier in the day I wouldn't even allow myself to consider the thought, now I find myself really wanting it to be true. I still have no idea what I will ask for. What is it that I truly want more than anything else?

As I look towards the Man, I see Him down on His knees. The woman who is next in line has apparently collapsed on the stairs as she approached Him. I can tell she is crying as she holds her face in her hands. I watch once again, as this gentle Man takes the woman by the elbows and helps her to her feet and to the platform. As He guides her over to the large chair, He draws her into His lap as He takes a seat. He sits there holding her and waits as she continues to cry, desperately trying to regain her composure so that she can tell Him what it is that has her so broken. Almost everyone I have seen has sat in the Man's lap, which once again brings the comparison to Santa Claus to my mind. I have noticed a few who did not take a seat, but even they seemed to have the same glow on their face as they left as everyone else. For some, it seemed all they needed was a hug and to hear Him say that He loved them. For others, their hearts seemed to be extremely burdened. Those weren't people with just desires and dreams; those were the ones with definite needs. Odd, how everyone whom I have watched leave did seem to be completely satisfied with what they received. But wait! Everyone had walked away with nothing in their hands. How could that be? At least Santa always had a large sack of toys and treats to hand out. How was it that this Man is meeting needs and fulfilling dreams if He has nothing to give them? Just what exactly is it He has to offer?

The closer I get to the front of the line, the more I find myself reflecting back on my childhood. Why is it I never felt loved or valued? Oh, don't get me wrong. I know my parents loved me. They had to. They adopted me. I always seemed to be quick to point a finger at my birth mother for my feelings of inadequacy and thinking nobody loved me. I reasoned that if the person who gave birth to me wanted nothing to do with me and didn't love me, nobody else could. Or maybe it was just me. My siblings were also adopted and they never seemed to struggle with this. My one sister told me that being adopted proved to her how much she was loved by our parents because she was chosen. My childhood wasn't filled with happy times and close family situations, or at least I had no memories of that. Friendships were always difficult for me and I never seemed to fit in. When others were choosing teams, I was never picked towards the head of the team. True, I was seldom picked last. It always seemed as if my place in line and being chosen had more to do with me as a person rather than my ability at whatever we were choosing teams for. It was more of a statement that I was "weird" rather than not a good player. Team captains didn't always choose the best player, they chose the popular kids or their friends and therefore I generally got picked towards the middle. Though I wasn't the last one picked, the message that I wasn't "one of the gang" came through loud and clear. Sometimes the middle can feel just as lonely as the end. I always felt like there must be something wrong with me that made it difficult for me to feel like I fit in. Even if by some odd chance I got to be one of the captains who got to pick the teams, it was as if the first couple kids would be disappointed to have to be on my team. Everything and everyone around me seemed to be screaming at me: "failure," "inadequate," "stupid," "ugly," etc. After a number of years of repeatedly hearing the same thing over and over, I began to believe them and concluded that everyone couldn't be wrong, so I must be a pretty lousy person.

As I moved into the teen years, friends were still very hard to come by. I was friendly and tended to be outgoing when it came to sports and things like that. I was a part of many groups and teams, but I never felt like I belonged. I was good in band and received many awards, yet found myself often wondering if anyone would even notice if I wasn't there. I was good at basketball, but it seemed that the coaches had their ideas of what they wanted to do and I didn't seem to be a part of their plans. I would have students from other schools asking me why I didn't play more, and I had no answer to give them. It's almost as if my talent and abilities were more obvious to others outside of our school then they were to my own coaches. Even though that should have made me feel validated, it really didn't. We had good coaches, and if they didn't think I was good enough to play, then they obviously knew me better than other people did. I would go to school functions and dances after ball games, but I would always find myself sitting alone in a corner, not interacting with others. Nobody seemed to notice me there. No one ever approached me to invite me to join them and their group of friends. I must have been the most outgoing loner in our school. I can't think of a single time or single person who ever made me feel important or valuable. Knowing I was loved by my parents did very little to help me feel loved. After graduation and on through college I always lived by the philosophy "if you really knew me, you wouldn't like me". I also began believing that if I allowed myself to care about anyone they would either leave me or die. All of this combined led to a very lonely life.

I always felt the need to play the "game" and try to be everything others wanted or needed me to be. I never felt it was ok to just be myself. To do that would be to risk being ridiculed, judged and rejected. Plus, if hiding behind walls and wearing an array of masks got me acceptance and at least made me feel like other people liked me, then maybe the sacrifice of not being "real" was ok. However, I still couldn't risk caring about anyone without risking being hurt by the person either leaving or dying. I'm sure this stemmed from a number of losses in life; the death of my brother, close friends moving away. Somehow, I would personalize this sort of thing and make it about me. It wasn't safe to risk caring. Years of pretending to be someone I wasn't and keeping people at a distance was beginning to take its toll on me.

4

"What am I doing here?" I ask. Who do I think I am that this Man will care about what I want or what is important to me? Nobody else ever has! What a waste! I should just leave. I'm sure that everyone else here has more crucial needs than me and are more deserving of His time. As I consider walking away, I glance towards the platform one more time. It won't be long now till it is my turn. Can I really deal with my needs going unmet one more time? As I begin to turn, I notice the Man looking in my direction. Or am I just imagining that? I look at Him; there seems to be something in His eyes practically begging me to stay. I decide I really have nothing to lose at this point by staying, so even though I believe it will be a mistake, I stay.

What is it about this Man that seems to have so much control and power over me? I have had more than my share of "controlling" people in my life. I thought most of those days were behind me.

Twenty plus years of counseling should get me at least that much shouldn't it? I guess not. To walk away now would be nearly impossible. Oh, I could come up with all kinds of rational reasons for staying: i.e. I've been here all day; I am almost to the head of the line, so to leave now would mean I have wasted my whole day and for what? Plus, the fact that all the people whom I could see seemed to have found what it was they were looking for. It isn't the waiting that is making me want to leave, it is the chance of being let down or disappointed or rejected that has me wanting to leave.

"What do I want?" the question seems to be going through my head over and over repeatedly. The complication of this simple question continues to eat away at me. It practically haunts me. If I let my imagination go wild, I can think of all kinds of things that I want: a new car, a good job, a husband, the "perfect" life (2 kids, a dog and a house with a white picket fence). Those aren't things that I really need though. But the question isn't, "What do you need?" it is "What do you want?" Hmmm?? What do I want? I can get very philosophical and say that what I want is peace on earth, no more wars, no road rage, no more rude and obnoxious people, no school shootings, no rapes, no abuse, no murders. The interesting thing about that list is that is very "universal," not very personal. To try to think of something that I want for me is almost unthinkable. Too many years of thinking it is not all right to want anything. Too many voices yelling in my head telling me not to ask for anything, telling me that I am going to be let down, telling me it is wrong, telling me it is bad to ask, telling me that only bad girls ask for things.

I push the question out of my mind and work on shutting out the voices. I haven't even asked for anything yet. I try to focus on the other people in the line. So many people! I wonder what they came wanting. Will they get it? How many will walk away disappointed? Why do I think I am the only one unworthy of getting what I want? "Stop it!" I yell to myself. "Quit torturing yourself this way!" I go back to watching people. I scan the lines to see if I know anyone here today. Is this a one-day event, or did others receive an invitation with a different day and place? That seems unlikely based on the number of people here. As I look around I don't see anyone I know. I find myself glancing at the Man frequently. I try not to make it obvious because I don't want to risk Him seeing me looking at Him. But as the line continues to move I find it getting more and more difficult to take my eyes off Him. After all, He is the reason I am here. Why shouldn't I be watching Him?

As another person leaves the platform, I hear Him say once again, "I love you so much. Come back soon." For some reason, I believe that He means it every time He says it. I think some people tend to get into "ruts," and phrases such as "I love you" become more a part of a "routine," rather than actual term of endearment or affection, but not this Man. He appears to be genuinely concerned for every person He sees. There is no sense that He is just doing the "socially acceptable" thing and "making nice" by saying He loves these people. I haven't noticed one person leave that He didn't say this to. Were there any? Maybe I missed it while I was daydreaming. Who is this Man that is so full of love? Why is He here? What does He want?

I find myself fixed on this Man. I need to know more about Him. I need to figure out what He is really after. I need to know this is for real. I watch Him closely as one person after another goes up and sits on His lap and talks to Him. He listens intently to everyone. He watches them as they talk and wipes tears from their eyes or rubs their back or just holds them. There doesn't appear to be any routine that He goes through. He treats each one as an individual. He honestly seems to care for each man, woman and child He meets. Santa Claus never did that! With Santa it was more of a routine: sit on his lap, tell him what you want, be instructed to be good, be informed that he would be watching, get a toy and go on your way. One after another, it would be the same thing for everyone there. Not with this Man, He treats each person as if he or she were the only person there. He doesn't rush them. He doesn't keep looking at His watch (He doesn't even have a watch on). He doesn't seem distracted as some talk on and on. He is always attentive to the conversation. He never takes His eyes off the person He is talking to. He never scans the crowd to get an idea of how many people are still there. He never seems bored or uninterested. You would think that as you sit on His lap or talk to Him that you are the only one He cares about at that particular moment.

The line seems to be picking up speed, or is it just my imagination? The closer I get, the more nervous I get, the more I question if I really want to go through with this. What will happen if I get up there and still don't know what to ask for? Can I just say that anything He wants to give me will be fine with me? What if I am so nervous, I can't even say anything? I will be so embarrassed! This is just a disaster waiting to happen! I keep telling myself that I have nothing to lose. I feel deep within me that whatever happens today will be a life-changing experience. Will I embarrass myself so badly that I will never recover from it? I know I need some life-altering event; I just don't have any more strength or courage to continue on. Something has to change, and maybe that's what today is about; changing my life. But how can this Man do that? What is it He can offer that can so improve my quality of life?

The man seems to be so gentle. His voice has a natural calming effect, even if the only thing I can hear is "I love you so much. Come back soon." His eyes have an amazing peace in them. Nothing about Him comes across as threatening. Everything about this Man seems to personify love. How amazing that would be if it were to be true. Love personified! Can it be? I am familiar with some of the Bible and know that God is love, but God isn't a person, He is just God. I know that 1 Corinthians 13 talks about the characteristics of love; it says, "Love is patient, love is kind. It does not envy, it does not boast, it is not proud. It is not rude, it is not self-seeking, it is not easily angered, it keeps no record of wrongs. Love does not delight in evil but rejoices in the truth. It always protects, always trusts, always hopes, always perseveres. Love never fails" (I Cor. 13:4-8 NIV). Maybe that describes God, but it sure doesn't describe any person I know. People are all about "keeping record of wrongs" and most are very "self-seeking." Plus, let's face it, people will always fail you.

Only a few people left in front of me. It is too late to back out now without making it very obvious. Can you imagine what those in line around you would think? They would all think you are crazy to make it this far and then leave. The last thing you want is for people to think you are crazy. You aren't crazy! Maybe a little mixed up, but not crazy! You can feel yourself beginning to panic. You still have no idea what to ask for. What is it you actually want from this Man? Or is it more accurate to say that you don't know what would be safe to ask for in case you don't get it? Realistically, you will be much better off asking for something small and insignificant. That way if you don't get it, it is no great loss!

5

The woman with her two children steps up on to the platform. The children run over to the Man and jump into His lap. The woman, embarrassed by her children's behavior, quickly hurries over to the chair to grab them. She reaches for her children to have them stand up as she apologizes to the Man. But as she reaches for them, the Man draws them to Himself and takes the woman's hand in His. He looks her in the eyes and says, "Let the little children come to Me, and do not hinder them, for the kingdom of heaven belongs to such as these." She stops, lets go of her children and begins to sob. He waits for several seconds and then calls her by name, "Martha, it's all right. You did nothing wrong. You have done such a great job raising these two lovely children on your own with very little help. What you don't yet realize is that I love them more than you do. You have sacrificed much for their sake, but I gave My life for them — and for you. I love you more than you can know right now. Come, sit with us, and tell Me what it is I can do for you. What is it that you want?”

The woman stands there in shock; how does this Man know her name? How does He know so much about her life? Instead of being concerned about her children’s behavior, now she begins to be concerned about their safety. Are they safe with this Man? Who is He? Almost as if He can read her mind, He calmly speaks again, “You know who I am. Please, don’t be afraid. I will never harm a child; children are precious to me. Please, sit down. Let’s talk. The children are fine.”

“What do you mean I know who you are? I have no idea who you are or what it is you want with me,” she says.

“Don’t you have that wrong?” He asks. “This isn’t about what I want; this is about what you want. You and I haven’t talked in some time, but that was your choice. I will never force Myself on someone, but that doesn’t mean I’m not aware of what's going on in your life. I've seen you struggle. I've seen your tears at night when you think no one is around. I know how betrayed you feel by those who told you that they cared but left you. I have never left you. I never will," He assures her.

Confused, she just stands there staring at Him. He doesn't look familiar to her, yet there is something about His voice that is vaguely familiar. It is from a time long ago. She can't quite place it, but she knows it is nothing to fear. Slowly, she approaches Him and joins her children sitting in this gentle stranger's lap. As she does, it is like someone pushed the "mute" button because at that point, I can't hear another word of the conversation. She realizes where she knows Him from. A look of total shock crosses her face, followed by more tears. As they get up to go, He takes time to hug each one individually and as they head off the platform, once again I hear Him say, "I love you so much. Come back soon."

I watch the three of them walk off. The children are tired, but skipping and singing as they leave. The mother has tears streaming down her face, but it is different this time. This time there is a smile on her face, and I can tell that the tears are tears of joy. Like the others I have seen leave, she also seems to have a glow about her. I don't know how long I stand there watching them as they vanish into the crowd. As I stand there, lost in my thoughts, I hear a voice say, "Come to Me, I long for you." I look up and realize that the Man is looking straight at me and that it is He who has just spoken. I am next!! How could I forget that I am next? Instantly, panic takes hold of me.

I stand there and put my hand on the rail to go up the steps but it is as if my feet can't move. "Don't be afraid, Judy. I won't hurt you. It's ok, you are safe here," He gently speaks. I slowly move up the steps and onto the platform. He never gets out of His chair. He just sits there watching every step I take. "I see the fear in your eyes and I can sense the tension running rampant through your body. I wish I could come to you, but I don't want to scare you off. So I'll sit here with My arms open and wait for you to come to Me."

How can He tell so much about me? It's as if He knew me somehow. He never takes His eyes off me nor makes one motion towards me. He just sits there exactly as He said He would do. I continue up the steps and onto the platform. You would think I would feel as if I am on display and worried about what all the people still waiting are thinking of me, but somehow, I'm not sure how, it is as if there are only two people in the room, this Man and me. As I get a bit closer, He speaks once more, "Come to Me. Come sit on my lap. I so long to hold you close to Me. Come and talk to Me. I want to hear everything you have to say. Please tell Me. I understand your fears. Who can blame you for being afraid? But I promise you, you have nothing to be afraid of with Me."

I go over and stand next to Him. Am I safe here? The gentleness of His eyes and His voice are a thousand times more-so up close. He refrains from making any sudden or jerky motions. He sits very still. It is almost as if I am a deer and He knows that any movement from Him will make me turn and run. "I'm so glad you came. I wasn't sure if you would accept My invitation or not. I was so excited when I noticed you in line. Of course, there was a time or two when it seemed as if you might leave. Thank you for staying. I am sure that had to be extremely difficult for you. After all, what if this is all a joke and you are to be let down once again? Don't worry, that isn't going to happen. I promise. Won't you please come and have a seat? For such a long time I have looked forward to just holding you close to Me.

I still am not ready to trust this Man and sit on His lap. I stand next to the chair, watching Him closely to see if He is for real. I generally am pretty good at reading people, so if this guy is trying to fake me out or trick me in some way, hopefully I will be able to pick up on that before it is too late. “How do you know me?” I ask Him.

“You are My child. I have searched you and I know you. I know when you sit and when you rise; I perceive your thoughts from afar. I discern when you go out and when you lie down. I am familiar with all your ways. Before a word is on your tongue I know it completely. I have you hemmed in – behind and before; I have laid My hand upon you. Where can you go from My spirit? Where can you flee from My presence? If you go to the heavens, I am there. If you make your bed in the depths, I am there, if you rise on the wings of the dawn, if you settle on the far side of the sea, even there My hand will guide you, My right hand will hold you fast. I created your inmost being; I knit you together in your mother’s womb. You are fearfully and wonderfully made. Your frame was not hidden from Me when you were made in the secret place. When you were woven together in the depths of the earth, My eyes saw your unformed body. All the days ordained for you were written in My book before one of them came to be. You are so precious to Me. I promise to be there for you and lead you in the way everlasting," He says.

Dazed and confused, I stand there not knowing what to think or do. This is impossible. These things He is saying, there is no way that can be true. Or can it? It is almost as if I can see everything He said taking place. It is like watching a film of my life from before conception. How odd the whole thing seems to be. Thinking about what He said brings up some painful thoughts, thoughts about my birth mother. "Fearfully and wonderfully made"? Who is He trying to fool! I was nothing more than a mistake or worse yet a nothing. The more I think about this, the angrier I grow. This guy has no idea what He is talking about. She never wanted me. She never cared about me. She never even gave much thought to me once she was rid of me. The only "fear" involved in my conception and birth was the fear that she would get caught and someone would notice she was pregnant.

"Don't do that," He says as He interrupts my thoughts, "Don't blame Marie. Even if you are right about her not wanting you or thinking of you or caring about you, don't underestimate Me. Do you remember when Joseph was reunited with his brothers in Egypt and they were afraid of what he might do to them because they had sold him into slavery years before? Do you remember what he said to them? He said, 'You intended to harm me, but God intended it for good.' Marie didn't intend to harm you. She just made some poor choices. However, I knew what was going to happen before it did, and I intended it for good. Could I have stopped their union from conceiving? Yes. But I had plans for you. I needed you. Yes, Marie gave birth to you, but I created you. She may have given up her parental rights to you, but I have never done that. As I already said, you are My child."

"She didn't even remember when my birthday was!" I cry. "All she managed to accomplish was making her bad choices and problems my problems. She didn't want me, so she pushed me off onto someone else. Someone who supposedly wanted me, but now I have to wonder what it was they wanted me for."

"They did want you. They just didn't know how to be good parents. Nobody showed either of them what parenting was all about. Unfortunately, parenting isn't something that you just know naturally. You need to learn how to be a good parent. Their intentions were good. They knew they wanted to have children but were unable to conceive. I won't make excuses for their shortcomings and for the pain you ended up having to endure. There is no excuse for that. I'm so sorry for all that happened to you. But Judy, you were never alone. I was there. Every step of the way, I was there. You may not believe Me, but I never left you." As He speaks, I notice His eyes filling with tears.

"Who are you? What gives you the right to stand here and say I was never alone? You have no idea how alone I was and how alone I have been my entire life. What do you know about the pain I've endured? You don't know anything about my pain," I reply.

"You know who I am. 'What gives Me the right?' That's what you asked? I promised to never leave you or forsake you and I keep My promises. I will never leave you. I love you too much."

"What do you want with me? Why are you here? Why don't you just leave me alone?" I ask.

"I can't leave you alone. Oh, don't get Me wrong; I won't force Myself on you. I'm a firm believer in free will. I designed the concept. As to what do I want and why am I here, I think you know that. I've come to bind up the brokenhearted, to proclaim freedom for the captives, and release from darkness for the prisoners, to proclaim the year of the Lord's favor and the day of vengeance of our God, to comfort all who mourn, and provide for those who grieve – to bestow on them a crown of beauty instead of ashes, the oil of gladness instead of mourning and a garment of praise instead of a spirit of despair. What of that applies to you? That's why I'm here: I'm here to heal you and to set you free. Why are you here?"

"I don't know why I'm here. I actually threw the invitation away when I got it. I was so sure it was some scam. But then I was afraid to not come on the small chance that it might be for real. Even though I still have no idea what it is I want. I couldn't risk not coming. The possibility that there was someone who could truly 'fulfill my greatest desire, grant my wildest dream and meet my most desperate needs': how do I just ignore such an invitation? Not to mention that the first paragraph described me pretty well. I had to find out if it truly was all a lie," I said as tears streamed down my face.

"Judy, won't you please sit down. I'm not going to hurt you. I'm not going to take advantage of you. I'm not going to force myself on you. I just want to hold you. I want you to know what it is to truly feel safe. You asked Me what I wanted: that's what I want. I want you to be safe. I want you to feel safe. I want to hold you, protect you and keep you from all harm. I want you to know Me, not just know about Me or think that you know Me. I want you to know Me as I know My Father. So what is it you want? Please, come sit down and talk to Me. You need to be heard. You have the right to be heard. I want to listen." As He says this, He sits very still and reaches His hand out to me.

Not knowing what else to do, I take His hand, go to Him and slowly sit down. He carefully puts His hand on my shoulder. I can sense He is aware of my fear. "Are you ok?" He inquires. "Don't be afraid. You really are safe."

"Safe? I don't even know what it is to feel safe! How can you say I'm safe?" I question.

"Do you trust Me?" the Man asks.

"I want to trust You. I want to believe that what You say is true. I want to feel safe," I assure Him. "But I'm afraid. I'm afraid to believe. I'm afraid to trust. I'm afraid to risk it. How do I know You haven't just hacked into my computer and found out a bunch of stuff about me? That You haven't been reading my emails and that You really are who I think it is You are claiming to be?"

"What can I do to assure you I'm not a computer hack?" He asks with a slight chuckle. "I've been accused of being a lot of things, but not that. How can I put you more at ease and convince you that I truly am God? I really do want to free you and heal you! I know the plans I have for you. Plans to prosper you and not to harm you, plans to give you hope and a future. I know how hard it is for you to risk hoping for anything. 'Hope' for you is truly a 'four-letter word.' It breaks my heart that hope is such a scary thing for you."

"What plans? What are Your plans for me? What kind of future? What do you mean by 'prosper'? Are you going to pay off my credit card debt? Is that it?" I ask.

"I'm sorry, but you aren't quite at a place where I can tell you what the plans are. I will make them clear to you, but not right now. So let Me ask you; if you weren't sure what my plans for you were, then why did you give up your plans when I asked you to?" He asks.

"I'm not sure. Because I knew it was the 'right' thing to do, I guess. Plus, You gave me five months to think about it once You asked me. When I asked You what I would get if I did as You asked, You made it clear that I would never know that until after I let it go. So that's what I did. Why? Was it just a test? I really didn't have to give up my plans?" I ask impatiently.

6

Giving up my plans had not been an easy thing for me. After years of feeling life wasn't worth the effort and believing I would be better off dead, I had finally made the decision to end my life. I had determined the essentials of where, when and how. I made the necessary purchases and everything was set. All I needed to do was wrap-up some business matters and wait for the selected day. This time I had every intention of going through with it, until God asked me to give up my plans for His. That was a long time ago. At first, I said no. It had taken me years to get to a place where I was willing to take my life. I wasn't just going to give that up! I made a compromise and agreed to put my plans "on-the-shelf." Five months later, I agreed to give them up. To now think that it was some sort of "test" was too much to take in.

"No, it was not a test. I don't work that way. But then, you know that," He replies. "Now I do use creative tactics at times. I also take advantage of events and places to speak to people where they least expect it. Like speaking to you through songs on the radio at just the right time. Or billboards on corners that you pass all the time and that you will be passing again. I thought that was a rather clever idea on my part, didn't you? It definitely got your attention, which was the whole point."

"I will have to admit, that was pretty clever. To turn a corner and see in huge letters "Jesus loves you. Repent and believe." It did get my attention. I even went back the next day to take a picture of it and to sort of make sure it was real and not just some weird hallucination the night before," I inform Him.

"I know you did. I thought that was kind of cute," He chuckles. "Do you still have the picture?

Actually, I had hung on to the picture. In fact, not only did I hang on to it, but I also made several copies of it (just in case.) It seemed so obvious now that God had been pursuing me for some time. The odd way certain songs would be on the radio at just the "right" time. I would see a billboard that seemed to "appear" out of nowhere. I would get a call from a friend when I really needed it. I would visit churches and the sermon would be the very thing that I had been struggling with. Or the time I was caught off guard by an unexpected hug at a women's retreat. All of these things and more now seemed to be coming together in a giant mural that showed He hadn't given up on me and had continued to pursue me.

My thoughts take me away to that women's retreat. The whole weekend had been significant in so many ways and I hadn't even wanted to go. I was so glad I had. A good friend had asked me a question before the retreat but I wouldn't answer it. She had asked me if there was one thing that could prove to me that God loved me, what would it be? I didn't even have to think about it; I knew the answer. Afraid that if I shared the answer with her it could be "arranged" to take place, I refused to tell her. However, during the retreat she came to me and shared with me she knew what it was and she did. We talked about the different ways that might play out and what that might look like. At the end of the retreat they had roses for all the ladies. As the women made their way out of the room I watched the women who were handing out the roses. They would greet each lady and chat a bit, hand her a rose and then move on to the next person. When I went to take my rose, the woman gave me a hug and said she was really glad I came. I walked away puzzled because I was the only one she had hugged. I had to wonder if this was just one step towards the "one thing."

"Can I ask you something, Judy?" He softly asks. "Will it be ok, if I hold you now? I don't want to make you uncomfortable, but I really do want to hold you in my arms and just draw you close to Me. Isn't that what you really want? Didn't you once say that to be embraced in such a way would be the 'one thing' that would convince you that I love you? Or is that why you don't want Me to hold you; will it be too big a risk for you to take in case it isn't that 'one thing' that will convince you?" He asks.

I have to think about that. Can He be right? Is that why I don't want Him holding me? No, that isn't it. It's because anytime someone has held me there always seemed to be other "unspoken" expectations. I realize this Man has stumbled onto something that I truly do want; I want to feel loved. Feel it in such a way that there is no doubting it. Feel it in such a way that the reality of it overrides any doubts I have about my inability to receive love. To be so saturated with feeling loved that all I feel is love. To be consumed with love and only love. To be so lost in that experience that it surpasses any vision or idea that even the best love story could try to conjure up. That is what I want. I want to know that I know that I know what love is.

"I'm not quite ready for that yet. I can't say that you are totally wrong in why I'm hesitant, but it is complicated. Yes, you are right; it is a tremendous risk for me to take. And yes, I did say that being embraced and feeling loved would be the 'one thing' to convince me. But I still have questions and there are still so many things that have me baffled," I said, "for starters where were You when I was with Dana? Or where were You during the all night prayer? Or should I start at the beginning and ask where You were when I was abused? Why would You allow that to happen to me? How could You just stand by and not do anything? Why didn't You help me? I begged You to help me, but You never did. Why did You let them hurt me? Why wouldn't You just let me die?" I cry. As I ask these intense questions, I begin sobbing uncontrollably.

Almost naturally, I wrap my arms around this Man and cry on His shoulder. He slowly wraps me in His arms and quietly whispers to me, "I'm so sorry you had to endure all that. Dana was supposed to show you what a true friend was. She was to be there to comfort you and support you, to help you recover. She was to show you My love and to be there for you after the loss of your brother. Dana 'dropped the ball!' She let her own selfish desires get in the way. I tried talking to her. I begged her to stop, but she wasn't interested in listening. It both angered Me and broke My heart when she tried convincing you that I understood and that it was ok with Me."

"She was the adult Sunday school teacher. How could she say You understood? That never made sense to me, but I assumed she knew better than I did. To say it was 'ok?' She was married!! That should never be ok!" I exclaimed.

"She knew that was a lie. She lied to you, she used you and on top of that she continued the cycle of emotional abuse that had you questioning your identity," He explained.

"She knew I was confused; I had confided in her. I told her things I had never told anyone. She knew my deepest, darkest fears and secrets," I assured Him.

"She used your trust in her against you. She took advantage of you," He said as He continued to try and comfort me.

"Why would she do that?" I ask.

"She was lying to herself too. She was trying to justify her actions. I do believe she cared for you, however, she chose a terrible way to try and show that," He answered.

When my brother died I was consumed with regrets. I wondered if there was some way I could have prevented his death. Dana and her husband Phil invited me to stay with them for awhile; to give me time to grieve. She knew how vulnerable I was.

"You're right," He said, "she did. She betrayed your trust in so many ways. I wish she would have listened to Me. She was wrong. What do you want Me to say?"

I'm not sure what I want Him to say. I thought Dana was the best friend I ever had. She gave me a shoulder to cry on. She would listen to me for hours as I poured out my pain and grief. She enjoyed spending time with me. When a woman at church judged me, Dana defended me. She made me feel important and special. This was something new to me.

We had Bible studies together, made late-night pizza runs and I played softball on the same team as Phil. The three of us were like family. At least that was how it seemed. We would play games, watch movies and stay up for hours discussing current topics in the news or local happenings. Staying with them had given me a sense of safety and security.

“That’s what I wanted for you; a place you could feel safe and accepted,” He said. Once again, He knew what I was thinking. “The day Dana decided to do things her way was a dark day. She also betrayed Me that day.”

The events of that dreaded day still confuse me. Dana and I had been home alone. It was an especially hard day for me. The grief I felt was at an extremely high level. As she had done so many times before, she held me and let me cry. But on that day, she took it a step further and crossed the line between “friend” and something else. At first I wasn’t aware of what was happening. She continued to hold me close and assure me that everything was ok. When I realized what was happening, I was shocked. Confused, I tried to pull away. Nothing about this seemed “ok.” Our involvement grew from that point on.

I look into the Man’s eyes. “I didn’t know what to do. I was afraid if I said no she might kick me out. Or worse, that she would no longer want to be my friend,” I said. “I didn’t want to risk losing that, so I went along with her.”

“Judy, I understand,” He assured me. “Dana knew right from wrong. She knew she had crossed a line. Not only was she older than you, but she also had a position of authority as your Sunday school teacher. She is accountable for her actions. She was the teacher. She was the married one. She gave you a place to stay. She was wrong!” There is so much love in His eyes as He speaks to me. It's almost too much for me to handle. I feel so guilty and so unworthy.

I could have told Dana "no." I should have. I was afraid, but that is no excuse. As I think about this, I remember when evidently the guilt and shame became too much for her to deal with and she said we had to stop. Even though she never directly said it was my fault, I felt as if she was implying it was. She had me feeling as if I was responsible.

"Judy, listen to Me," He says. "She manipulated you into thinking that it was you who had corrupted her. She was living in denial. Then Phil got a new job and they moved away. You felt so abandoned. I intended it to be so different. She was suppose to help you through the hard times and encourage you to lean on Me. Instead, she helped build the wall between us."

He was right about that! There had been no contact with Dana in over 20 years, yet there were times when it felt like yesterday. It was years later when I realized I had been used. She used her friendship and her position in the church to gain my trust and then used it against me. We had kept in touch for awhile after they moved, but things between us were never the same. She continued to try and distance herself from our involvement.

As I look at this Man who is holding me, I see so much clearer how Dana had contributed to the walls between Him and me. He was right about her. How she had used me, abused me and then abandoned me. I was left holding all the blame, guilt and shame. I couldn't help but wonder how different my life would have been if she had listened to Him and been the friend He had intended for her to be.

The tears keep coming. "Ok," I say, "so what about the all-night prayer thing?"

"The all night 'prayer' ordeal: (and I use the term 'prayer' loosely) should never have happened to you. They were so wrong in what they did. They used you. They owed you an apology. They owed you a lot more than that! Once again, they made you feel as if there was something wrong with you. I still get angry when I see the effects of that night continuing to come between us. Let Me assure you, I worked throughout that night to keep you safe. Judy, I'm so sorry that so much of what has happened to you has been at the hands of people claiming to be My followers. I'm sorry you were hurt so badly. I am utterly crushed that you couldn't tell I was there with you; instead you felt all alone. I tried to let you know. You have no idea how it hurt me to have to watch what was done to you. I was so angry! I wanted to kill them for hurting you. I wanted to call down a thousand angels to your defense and just obliterate all of them. You have no idea how badly I wanted to do that," He says trying to maintain His composure.

"Why didn't you?" I cry. "I was held down against my will for over eight hours by four grown men! I went home with bruises on my wrists from their grip. How was I supposed to explain this happened while being prayed for?

I was so angry and so scared. Why didn't you do something?"

"I couldn't do that. They needed to have a chance to know Me. I gave them free will; I couldn't very well kill them for using it. I tried reasoning with them, to get them to stop — but it was no use. They refused to listen. But I did do something. When you were a child, I gave you the tools you needed to survive. I gave you the power to dissociate. I helped you to create parts who would make you feel safe, who would protect you, who would take the pain for you. Parts that could help you reason out even the most unimaginable things. Parts that needed to be loved and cared for. Parts that would hold all the rage that you so rightfully felt, so that it wouldn't totally consume you. I helped these parts care for you because you wouldn't let Me close enough to you. I gave you what you needed to make it through then and to make it through things later in life like that terrible night. I couldn't make the other people stop or leave you alone, but I could make sure that you survived," He tries to explain.

"I'm so angry at You," I tell Him. "I spent most of my life wishing I were dead. I so badly wanted to blame You for most of the things that happened to me. I needed someone to blame, and I was getting tired of blaming myself. I knew it was entirely my fault though, and that I was only getting what I deserved. I never meant to be bad."

"Please stop!" He pleads. "Don't say those things. Judy, My precious child, you were never bad. It wasn't your fault. Please, listen to Me — it was never your fault. I don't blame you for being angry with Me. I can understand why you would blame Me. The people who hurt you either said I made them do it or else they said I wanted them to do it! They lied to you! So many people have lied to you. They were the grown-ups; they knew what they were doing was wrong. When you were a child, you were too little to protect yourself. It wasn't your fault! None of what happened was ever your fault!"

7

Can this be true, I wonder. Is it possible that it was never my fault? I lift my head off His shoulder and look deep into His eyes: is He lying to me? He gently takes my face into His hands and looks me square in the eyes as He slowly whispers, “It wasn’t your fault.” Over and over He repeats those words. I want to run, to just break away and disappear. He has to be wrong. It has to be my fault. Who else could be at fault? They only did what they had to because I was bad. They had to show me what happened to little girls who were bad. As all these thoughts go racing through my head, the Man keeps repeating, “It wasn’t your fault. It wasn’t your fault. You aren’t bad. You never were bad. They lied to you. They lied to you your entire life. Please believe Me; it wasn’t your fault!” He seems almost desperate for me to believe Him. Believing Him sounds terrifying to me. How can I have been wrong so long and believed lies my entire life? Is this really possible? I am not sure I can allow myself to believe this.

As He continues to repeat, “It wasn’t your fault,” it is as if I can sense something starting to crack, like an unseen fortress; a barrier the size of a huge dam. It is as if I can see great floods of feelings beating against the firm foundation of this structure, beating at it again and again with what the Man is saying. Cracks in the structure start to appear. The cracks are small to begin with, almost invisible. However, as He repeats the phrase over and over, the cracks get larger. Feelings as strong as a mighty river continue to build up and beat against the lies that built this dam. Lies such as: I was bad. I was unlovable. I was stupid. I was crazy. The lie Dana had me believing that what happened was my fault. The prayer night convincing me that something was wrong with me or that I was evil. That everything was my fault. Lie after lie had built this mighty dam. A fortress that had in some ways protected me (or at least I thought it had) and that always had seemed impenetrable. Until now that is.

Soon, I can see the structure beginning to shake. There are places where water is beginning to seep through the wall. Chunks of concrete are being pushed out and broken off. What started out as small cracks are now gaping holes with water gushing through. Before I know what is happening, the wall collapses with a mighty flood destroying it. As the flood wipes out the dam, my heart breaks. I collapse into the Man's arms and continue to cry.

How could I have been so wrong all these years? How could I have blamed myself? How could I believe so many lies? I have so many questions.

I think the tears will never end. The pain is immense. I can't catch my breath. I can't stop crying. My whole body is racked with tremendous sobbing. Through all of this, He never lets go of me. He never stops comforting me. I realize that He too is crying as He gently rocks me in His arms. He then begins to sing to me. I recognize the song from church but I haven't heard it in a long time.

"You said You'd be there
and share all my sorrows,
You said You'd be there
for all my tomorrows;
I came so close to sending You away,
But just like You promised
You came there to stay.
I just had to pray!

And Jesus said,
'Come to the water, stand by My side,
I know you are thirsty, you won't be denied;
I felt every tear drop
when in darkness you cried
and I strove to remind you
that for those tears I died.

Your goodness so great I can't understand,

and dear Lord, I know that
all this was planned;
I know You're here now and always will be,
Your love loosed my chains
and in You I'm free;
But Jesus why me?
And Jesus said,
'Come to the water…'" (1.)

and the song sort of just faded away. It is for these tears He died.

As the Man continues to softly sing in my ear, I am aware of warmth slowly spreading through my body. I can't determine its origin but it seems to be accompanied by an overwhelming sense of peace. I have never felt such peace. I am no longer afraid. I am comfortable nestled in His arms. It feels so safe here. I now know exactly what it is to feel safe. I find myself wishing I could stay here for days and just be held. There is something else though, something I am having a more difficult time trying to identify. What is going on? It is as if everything about my life is changing. I had commented that I needed a life-changing experience, and I am in the process of having just that. Everything seems different! I now realize what else it is I am feeling; it is love. As I rest in the security and peace of this Man's embrace, love pours out of every inch of His being and totally consumes me. I know now I will never be the same.

As I continue to cry on this Man's shoulder and be held in His arms, gradually the immense power of grief is being transformed. It is as if the force of the flood is washing away all that has made me feel so dirty throughout my entire life. As the cleansing flood continues to wash over me, there is a sense of newness. I am not sure how to describe it or what exactly it is that I am feeling. No words are adequate to describe this overwhelming sensation. I feel clean, washed afresh, alive in a way that I have never experienced before. I am free!

“Thank you. Thank you so much,” I sob. “I can never thank you enough for all that you have given me today. More than I could have ever asked for. More than I could have ever imagined. More than I even knew I needed. Thank you so much.”

He looks me in the eyes and says, “No, Judy, thank you; thank you for coming today. Thank you for taking a chance. Thank you for being brave. I am so grateful that you came; that you stuck it out, that you didn’t leave when that would have been the easy thing to do. Thank you for trusting Me, for letting Me show you what it is that you have been missing. Thank you so much for giving Me a chance. I wasn’t sure you ever would, and I would have understood if you hadn’t. I’m just glad you did. You are so precious to Me. I love you so much. Come back real soon. Ok?”

EPILOGUE

As I get up to leave, I realize that so much has changed. For one thing, I believe Him; I believe that He loves me and that I am precious to Him. I believe that He means it each and every time He says it to everyone whom He has seen today. He truly is "love personified." But, of course, He is. He is God and God is love. The last verse of the song that He had been singing comes back to me. I begin singing the song as I step off the platform:

"Jesus, I give you my heart and my soul, I know that without God I'd never be whole; Savior, you opened all the right doors, and I thank you and praise you from earth's humble shores; take me, I'm yours." I realize this is truly the cry of my heart; I now know that "without God I'd never be whole."

As I begin to walk away, I wonder what it is that has made such a difference for me. Is it that He did indeed "fulfill my greatest desires, grant my wildest dreams and meet my most desperate needs" that has made the difference? What is it that I actually received from Him? I don't know where to start in attempting to answer that question, I have received so much. He bound up my broken heart. He proclaimed freedom to my captive soul and released it from the darkness of guilt and shame. He proclaimed the year of the Lord's favor and the day of vengeance of our God. He comforted me. He bestowed on me a crown of beauty instead of ashes, the oil of gladness (full of myrrh) instead of mourning, and a garment of praise, and He threw away the pitiful spirit of despair. Is it all of that which has made such a drastic difference? Oh, that was all very big and very life changing, but that isn't it. That isn't what makes the difference. Never again will I feel alone. Never again will I wonder if someone can ever love me. I am loved and I know that I am. The one thing that makes all the difference in the world and in my life is simply that — it is the "one thing." It is the gift of His embrace.

(1.) "For Those Tears I Died", by Marsha J. and Russ Stevens, copyright 1972

Additional copies of

The Gift of His Embrace can be purchased

at www.~~createspace.com/3710216~~

amazon.com

To contact Judy, you can email her at:
JCarson125@gmail.com

Made in the USA
Charleston, SC
31 October 2011